THE GRAPHIC ART OF
JAKOB
STEINHARDT

THE GRAPHIC ART OF
JAKOB
STEINHARDT

With a Critical Appreciation by
HAIM GAMZU

769
5

THOMAS YOSELOFF

NEW YORK   *LONDON*   *TORONTO*

© 1963 by A. S. Barnes and Company, Inc.

Library of Congress Catalog Card Number: 61-13932

Thomas Yoseloff, *Publisher*
11 East 36th Street
New York 16, N. Y.

Thomas Yoseloff, Ltd.
123 New Bond Street
London W.1, England

Printed in the United States of America
8799

CONTENTS

JAKOB STEINHARDT

A CRITICAL APPRECIATION by Haim Gamzu

Jakob Steinhardt has been living in Jerusalem since 1933. Although the tragic events of World War II were responsible for uprooting him, they also, paradoxically, played a large part in his rebirth as an artist. He had loved the Bible for many years, and the land of the Bible and its prophets lived in his imagination. Emigration to Jerusalem meant a renewal for Steinhardt—he was at last in an environment in which he felt a real sense of belonging, where his particular kind of imagination and gifts could fuse, take root, and flower.

By the choice of his themes Steinhardt is a Jewish artist. The aesthetic value of his work, his technical accomplishments, and the spiritual message of his creations make him a universal artist. His art is thoroughly human. He is not one of those who lock themselves away in an ivory tower and look at the world from a height of splendid isolation. He is a man concerned with humanity, anxious over its future.

Steinhardt's work is a variation on the eternal theme: the human condition. One of his first pictures shows an old man, sick, feeble, bedridden. This man was Steinhardt's grandfather, painted by the artist when he was fifteen years old. The sadness of the flesh and the sorrow of the spirit are themes to which the artist returns again and again. Longing for the beauty of life that springs from deep sadness, love for the human being, and despair at seeing vanity triumph: these elements are reflected in nearly all his artistic creations.

Steinhardt is a man of strife and struggle, of longing, deep feeling, and great understanding. He does not shun reality, but believes in an art that provokes thought. His art reveals his personality, his doubts, fears, and joys. He is not afraid to express an idea in his pictures. He believes that the message imparted by a work of art enhances its artistic value, that the work is more important than the artist. He has never ceased to improve his technique and he continues to search for new and better means of expression. One of the best and most important graphic artists of our generation, he feels deeply that technical virtuosity cannot atone for shallowness in a work of art, for absence of thought. This, indeed, is his credo. He does not belong to a school and cannot be classified under any "ism." Except for a short period in his life—the "Pathetic" period (1914–1921)—he has never identified himself with any groups or ideological movements. He has struggled with himself in his own studio, seeking and finding ways and means of self-expression.

When Steinhardt considers a theme important because of the problem it presents and its message to humanity, he uses every pictorial means at his disposal to express it. The result is a synthesis of artistic form and metaphysical meaning. In other words, in Steinhardt's handling of any human theme, there is the graphic presentation of an idea, which explains why the artist often prefers drawing to oil painting. His life is dedicated to the presentation of the human being and the infinite variety of things of which life consists. Steinhardt has never adopted the slogan *l'art pour l'art*, but has always given priority to the principle that the true purpose of art is to serve humanity.

Jakob Steinhardt was born in the little town of Zerkow on May 24, 1887. Most of the inhabitants of the town were Polish, with hardly more than a handful of Germans—officials mainly, and a small Jewish community. Zerkow was a forgotten little town, far from the main roads and railways. As long as his grandparents were alive, Steinhardt's father and mother still observed the Jewish festivals. But when they died, religious observance became lax, and the household no longer possessed that peculiar content with which tradition inspired Jewish family life in the Golah. But the little town, its houses and hovels huddled together like human beings for warmth, remained deeply engraved in the memory of the boy.

Steinhardt's interest in art began at a very early age. Whenever he got hold of illustrated journals he spread them out on the floor, lying for hours studying the smallest details of the battles, the units of cavalry and infantry, the steaming field kitchens, the makeshift hospitals, the officers' billets, the lines of recruits holding their tin and copper utensils, waiting patiently for their rations—which filled their pages. He listened avidly to the tales of war told by hoary veterans and retired officers, and his dearest ambition was to command a unit of soldiers. In the meantime, however, he had to rest content with the command of his neighbors' children, who willingly submitted to the yoke of discipline he imposed upon them in his unrelenting campaigns against an imaginary foe.

His carefree childhood came to a sudden end. When he was barely nine years old he was sent to a high school in Berlin and had to accustom himself to the harsh discipline of the school dormitory. He suffered much from homesickness, and eager expectation of the school holidays constituted practically the sole pleasure of his life. In 1900 his father died and his mother had to bring up two daughters and two sons. To this day the figure of his mother bent over the account books of the store until late at night remains an enduring memory. The death of his father deepened the boy's sense of responsibility towards himself and his studies. But the tedious lessons he learned at school could not compete with the exploits of the legendary heroes of the Greek epics, whose timeless struggles among themselves and with the all-powerful gods filled his fantasy. Jakob began to write—not adventure stories, but love poems. He was no more than thirteen years old, but the estrangement he felt from the practical world about him grew progessively stronger and his interest in his studies correspondingly weaker. He sought refuge in museums and art galleries, where he had discovered a world of line and color in the works of great artists, past and present.

Boecklin on the one hand, Rembrandt on the other, constituted the twin focuses of his interest, and the hours he spent contemplating their pictures were hours of true happiness. But he soon had to think seriously of his future. The portfolios filled with his own drawings had grown fatter and fatter. His mother regarded his strange preoccupation with concern, for his devotion to art had long ceased to be a hobby. Carefully she had preserved the drawings and one day dispatched a bundle of them to the curator of the museum in the town of Posen. Professor Kaemmerer's enthusiastic response placed her in a quandary. Before deciding whether to encourage her son on the course he had chosen or to persuade him to choose a more practical career, she sent his pictures to the famous painters Max Liebermann, Wilhelm Trübner and Lovis Corinth. Their replies put all her doubts at rest. She succeeded in bringing her son's talent to the notice of certain Maecenases in Posen, who, influenced by the favorable opinions of the renowned artists, resolved to help young Steinhardt continue his studies.

New horizons now opened before the young man. Paris, the "City of Lights," beckoned him. But before he set forth he had to master the art of drawing. He spent a year, constantly sketching, in the Berlin School of Handicrafts. Then he was accepted as a pupil by Lovis Corinth, from whom he learned the mysteries of color. But every hour that he could snatch he spent in the studio of Herman Struck, who taught him the art of etching. It was only after these three years of intensive preparation that he felt himself ready for Paris.

Steinhardt came to Paris in 1909. His first encounter with the city was not encouraging. The grimy houses, the pale men and women he saw in its crowded streets, the language that rang so alien in his ears, all combined to depress him. It was all so different from the colorful pictures of the Impressionists he had seen in the museums! He followed Corinth's advice and enrolled in the Académie Julien for the course of Jean-Paul Laurence, who had been the teacher of Corinth himself. Some days went by before the young artist made the acquaintance of the venerable master. The first encounter was depressing, even offensive. Laurence was examining the work of his pupils. He came up to Steinhardt's drawing board, examined the nude upon which the young man had been working, and commented, "Not bad! Not bad." Then he asked, "Are you a Spaniard?" "No," replied Steinhardt; "I am a German." Laurence turned his back upon him abruptly, without adding a word.

Perhaps it was because of the rankling unpleasantness of this first meeting that Steinhardt soon left the Académie Julien, but in any case he had been annoyed and distracted by the constant noise and tumult within its walls. The young artist decided to confine himself to drawing lessons in the Grande Chaumière in the evenings and later entered Matisse's studio as a pupil. But though Matisse was an excellent teacher, Steinhardt's dissatisfaction persisted and within a month he had joined the Académie Colarossi, where he continued his studies under Steinlen.

Gradually Steinhardt settled down in Paris, absorbed its Bohemian atmosphere, made friends with the younger artists, with whom he would drink a cup of coffee or a glass of wine and argue vociferously about the problems of art, about exhibitions, schools, and "isms." He felt completely at home in this world in which daring experiments were being made and new trends fostered. But his scholarship expired and he was compelled to return to Berlin, before he had sated his appetite for Paris. Here he saw his former teacher Corinth and submitted to him the work done in Paris. Corinth's reaction was reserved. Young Steinhardt, feeling frustrated, began to doubt whether the year in Paris had been well spent. After a year in Berlin wanderlust seized him again, and he crossed the Alps for a visit to Italy.

In Paris, as a matter of course he visited the Louvre and other museums, but mainly what had interested him was the Parisian "kitchen," in which new movements were taking shape and developing, often far too rapidly, into schools.

Italy of those years just before World War I was different. There, too, the younger artists were in a ferment, but the weight of tradition, the rich treasures of generations past, deeply impressed young Steinhardt and subdued the interest in new trends which his stay in Paris had induced. He immersed himself completely in a study of the works of the great masters which covered the walls of the Pitti and Uffizi galleries and which inspired the more peaceful mood of which he was so much in need after the shock and exhilaration of Paris. The cold reception Corinth had accorded to the paintings he had brought with him from Paris had perplexed him. He had felt lost, but nevertheless appreciated that the Olympian calm of the Renaissance giants was no longer in harmony with the storm-tossed spirit of twentieth-century man. He felt that the contemporary artist could no longer remain satisfied with classic beauty, with an art so sure of itself, when the clouds that were gathering over Europe, the uncertainty as to what the morrow might bring, the saber-rattling on both sides of the Rhine, could not but be reflected in the souls of the artists of the time. The doubts he entertained regarding himself, his mercilessly critical attitude towards the work he had done in Florence, so depressed him that one day he destroyed all his pictures. There was a dark emptiness within him. He could not bear the tranquility of Florence any longer. He left for Rome, his stations en route being the little towns of Umbria whose names are as beautiful as the countryside in which they are set—Orvieto, Assisi, Perugia. . . . During his short stay in Rome he met the artists of the city, to whom he unburdened himself of the doubts that oppressed him, secretly cherishing the hope that someone would contradict him, would try to prove him wrong. But he heard no word of encouragement. He returned to Germany eager for some new message, some new faith to guide him past the pitfalls that confronted the world of his generation. Slowly one thing emerged clearly out of his perplexity and confusion. He could not paint without conveying some message. If he succeeded in silencing his internal torment, he would devote himself to painting with dramatic content.

It was in this period that he made the acquaintance of the painter Ludwig Meidner. The latter, like Steinhardt, was dissatisfied with his own work and with contemporary art. He, too, was groping to find the right way in the labyrinth of different tendencies and schools. After many nightly strolls in the streets of Berlin and many long talks and discussions, their mutual liking and understanding grew into solid friendship, a friendship that was also based on common interests and a similar outlook on life. The link between them was their sincere desire to accomplish their mission as artists. Theirs was not the flippant, bohemian approach to the art of painting. They were disgusted with academic formality and stiffness, yet they were not drawn

12

towards the furious anti-academic reaction, as represented seven years earlier by a group called "Die Brücke" (The Bridge). At that time, in 1912, this group was already in a state of disintegration.

Steinhardt and Meidner decided to organize a group of artists for whom not form but drama, the evocation of thought and emotional reaction, was the essence of painting. They called their group "Die Pathetiker." After a short time they were joined by other young artists, including Ludwig Janthur, who already enjoyed something of a reputation in artistic circles in Berlin. A number of young poets and writers possessed of a similar urge towards pathos formed a parallel group which they called "Die Neo-Pathetiker." Together the two groups issued a monthly journal, *The New Pathos*, among whose contributors were the poetess Else Lasker-Schüler and Paul Zech.

These were the years in which Steinhardt found himself and developed a plastic language of his own, one that expressed not only pathos but resurgence, negating a world in disintegration under the impact of the new dangers threatening the human race. It was the *cri de coeur* of the individual, a manifesto of rebellion against the materialistic order. Stylistically, the broken lines, the elongated anatomical deformation of his work, were reminiscent of the Gothic. The stormy skies enhanced the sense of drama. This treatment was common to most members of the group. Meidner painted apocalyptic themes, while Steinhardt immersed himself in the Bible and conceived "The Prophet," elevated far above the suffering human multitude. Steinhardt was accorded the moral support of his friends, and when Hervard Walden, editor of *Sturm*, heard of his work, he visited Steinhardt's studio and decided on the spot to organize an exhibition of the "Pathetics"—Steinhardt, Meidner, and Janthur —in the art gallery of *Sturm*. The attitude of the critics to the exhibition, however, was devastating, and someone even referred to the "pathetic trio" as "exaggeration-loving, immature youths."

The movement was short-lived. But not divergencies of opinions or quarrels separated the artists. World War I broke out and dispersed the trio. Later they were to be referred to as "the only important group of expressionists in Berlin before 1914." As late as 1959, an article appearing in London quarterly *Painter and Sculptor*, written by Edouard Roditi, treated the "Berliner Pathetiker" at length.

At the beginning of the war Steinhardt was drafted into the German army and sent to the battle front in Lithuania. There, for the first time, he came into contact with small Jewish communities steeped in tradition whose way of life was utterly different from any he had known in Germany. There he saw true faith, a people living in poverty yet leading a rich spiritual life.

He saw them carrying on their backs the wares they peddled. Crushed and haunted by perpetual fear of an uncertain tomorrow, but despite all that, relishing the fulfillment of the prescriptions of their religion, come Sabbath or a holy day their countenance and entire aspect would change as if by magic; they were imbued with a genuine joy in their obedience to the Commandments of God. They diligently studied the Holy Scriptures, the source of life, the source of every wisdom.

The strong impression made on Steinhardt by this new experience gave him inspiration for many drawings. Working feverishly for long hours, he depicted the strange silhouettes of these people, showing their way of life, their occupations, their wearisome trudging through the narrow streets, their going about their daily occupations. He also showed how serenely they flocked to the houses of prayer, returning but slowly and reluctantly, as if wishing to prolong their communion with God.

In the poor little towns and villages of Lithuania he discovered some of the "Pathos" of which he had dreamed with his friend Meidner. He understood that these wretched-looking people were rich and happy despite their poverty. Did they not strive with all the might of their bodies and souls towards one end: the fulfillment of the will of God? They were conscious of their mission: to keep alive the spark of God.

If during his "Pathetic" days Steinhardt had discovered the Book, here in Lithuania he discovered the People of the Book. This revelation was Steinhardt's leading light in all his later life and work.

His artistic mission was to paint these people, to show a world plunged in fear and confusion that there still existed islands of faith; that there remained human beings whose lives had a meaning only in so far as they fulfilled their divine mission on earth.

Once he showed his drawings to a friend, an officer in the German army, who was so impressed with the dynamics and depth of feeling of the pictures that he persuaded the artist to send his work to the Berliner Secession. All the fifty drawings exhibited were sold at once. Two were purchased by his former teacher, Corinth, which was a matter of great pride for Steinhardt. The reviews were favorable, and he was called "a brilliant representative of the young generation of German painters." At the close of the exhibition, he was elected a member of the Secession.

Thus far the artist had been able to concentrate on his work and had had little experience of the hardships of army life or the perils of war. Then suddenly he was thrown into the midst of the fighting, and tasted all the bitterness, danger, and privation of the front-line soldier. Steinhardt's regiment was moved from Lithuania to the Balkan front. The German army was in a state of near disintegration. Supplies were irregular, and hunger and thirst, heat and dirt, lice and fleas, were the lot of the German soldier.

Steinhardt, who by then had contracted malaria, fainted by the roadside, was picked up by an ambulance and taken to a field hospital. Full of wounded, sick, and dying, the hospital was a living hell, and Steinhardt decided to get out while there was still a spark of life in his body. In the company of a Polish barber he set out on a life of vagabondage.

Cold and malaria completely wrecked Steinhardt's already poor health. His devoted companion had to steal food from retreating military units to hold off starvation. After innumerable adventures the two reached Sofia, where they boarded a train for Germany.

Sick and worn out, broken in body and spirit, he reached his mother's house. It took him a full year to recover from illness and depression, during which time he painted pictures that reflected his mood: "The Plague" and "Job."

It was also during this period that B. Neumann, the owner of the Graphisches

14

Kabinett in Berlin, decided to publish two collections of his etchings under the name *Dreams 1 and 2*. He also arranged Steinhardt's first one-man show, which drew flattering reviews from art critics and elicited much interest from collectors.

After his recovery, Steinhardt came more and more to regard the woodcut as "his" medium. He had been interested in it even in his "Pathetic" period. Now he found he loved the contact of the chisel with the live material, and being able to overcome the resistance of the wood gave him the satisfaction of having conquered matter. In the course of the cutting, he discovered unexpected possibilities for exploiting the texture of the medium, and found that the technique of the black-and-white woodcut based on strong contrast was the best way of recreating the forms that were firing his imagination and that gave him no rest. From 1929 on, he made hundreds of woodcuts, developing from an artist of talent to a virtuoso having deep sympathy for and insight into his subject matter as well as technical mastery.

For the Gurlitt Publishing Company he prepared a portfolio showing life in the Jewish towns as he had seen it in Lithuania. For the same house he also began to illustrate various books. His woodcuts were warmly welcomed, and materially his position improved greatly. He married Minni Gumpert, whom he had met at Gurlitt, and settled down to a quiet, productive family life. He continued to paint in oil, while concentrating on woodcuts. Important collectors purchased his works, and the number of his admirers grew steadily. As always, he rejected the concept of art for art's sake, and his pictures were full of ideas, which he succeeded in transmitting admirably through a sound technique and rich imagination.

But in 1933 this serenity and productivity was rudely disrupted. The Nazis came to power, and the persecution of the Jews began. Jewish intellectuals were arrested and thrown into prison or sent to concentration camps. One night an armed patrol of Nazi soldiers broke into Steinhardt's apartment and took him away. They interrogated him at great length and accused him of having disturbed with his wireless set a speech of the Führer. Fortunately, the officer who questioned him happened to be a sculptor, and the artist's name was well known to him. He gave orders for Steinhardt's immediate release and advised him to leave Germany at once.

A few days later, Steinhardt took his wife and small daughter and left Germany forever, leaving behind his paintings, drawings, and graphic work, only a portion of which was later returned to him. There was one place that Steinhardt knew he could turn to. Eight years before while visiting Palestine, he had made a number of friends. Now he would go there to live.

His Bible studies had revealed to him the universal meaning of the Book; in Lithuania he had found the People of the Book; in 1925, during his first visit to Palestine, he had discovered the land of the Bible, had set eyes on the age-old landscapes, and had become imbued with the holiness of Jerusalem. When he came to settle in Palestine, he rediscovered the Holy Land in all its grandeur and dramatic beauty.

Steinhardt established himself in Jerusalem and opened a drawing class in his studio; Jews and Arabs, Abyssinians and Armenians, Englishmen and Greeks flocked to his school and became devoted students and personal friends.

But, despite this, the initial period in Palestine was a very critical one for

Steinhardt. He had to absorb the landscape of the Bible, of Jerusalem. The blinding sunlight, the *hamsin* in the summer, the bleak, rocky contours of the wasteland, constituted stumbling blocks that he somehow had to surmount. Gradually he began to accustom himself to his new surroundings, to live with his environment, to penetrate beyond the envelope of sanctity, to comprehend the solemnity, the antiquity of Jerusalem. He became the lyric poet of its humble alleys, of its dignified sages and scholars, of the nobility of its beggars slowly plodding in the shadow of the ancient walls, treading the rough flagstones sanctified by generations of martyrs and saints.

He continued to paint in oil, but his principal medium remained the wood cut, which under his spell produced eloquent pages powerful in their sincerity and truth. However, he no longer remained content with black and white; he began to introduce color so as to reduce the tortured atmosphere of his early folios.

Steinhardt's integration in the life of Eretz Israel was primarily an internal process. He projected himself into the spirit of the objects he saw, into the trees and the stones. He revealed the spiritual richness of the dim figures moving under the arched doorways and along the narrow streets of Jerusalem, the rabbis, the *yeshiva* students and the pious Jews whose entire existence was circumscribed by the 613 *mitzvot,* who rejoiced in their godly heritage, the Torah, who seldom moved from their study of the Holy Books, who were raised to another, loftier, sphere with the arrival of the Sabbath.

His work was now a direct and logical sequel of his impressions of the Jews in Lithuania, but now he was an artist at the peak of his powers, a master of his medium, both ideologically and technically.

His brush and his chisel portrayed not only Jews, but also other inhabitants of the country—the Arabs, and principally the Bedouins, clad in their colorful robes within the monotony of Jerusalem, set off by the blinding sunlight. Into the wood he carved Bedouins at prayer, waiting expectantly for the dawn, resting in the shade of the lofty ramparts of the city. The present became an analogy of the past. He was preoccupied more and more with the Bible. He saw the great figures of the past not externally but as one who walked and talked with them. He made his woodcuts such a powerful means of expression that the close observer discovers in them not only the play of, and contrast between, light and shade, the debate between light and dark surfaces and the murmur of the delicate lines that reconcile them, but the radiance they emit, the reflection of the rich spirit of the artist, his sensitivity to mute suffering, which become articulate in his presence.

While Steinhardt was at work in Palestine, however, terror reigned in Central Europe. Millions of Jews were murdered. World War II was fought and unheard-of cruelties were perpetrated. The artist gave full rein to his imagination and drew and painted the horror that was consuming the world, creating likenesses of evil spirits and satanic creatures peeping out from a murky darkness, cynically mocking at man, jeering at everything he holds sacred.

Against these monsters and chimeric visions Steinhardt set the Prophet, who smothers with righteous anger the evildoer and the miscreant, but soothes and comforts the righteous and the pure in heart.

16

After the Jewish War of Independence, Steinhardt closed his private school and took over the Graphic Section of Bezalel, the Jerusalem School for Art and Arts and Crafts. During the years 1954–1957, he was director of this school. Though the administrative character of this post was not congenial to Steinhardt's artistic temperament, he raised considerably the academic standards of the school.

Yet he did not neglect his own creative work. The director of the Chicago Art Institute showed great interest in Steinhardt's woodcuts and, in 1951, organized a retrospective exhibition of his works which was very well received by the public and by art critics. This was Steinhardt's debut in America. In 1952, an exhibition of his prints took place in the Museum of Fine Arts in Boston; then followed exhibitions in the Smithsonian Institution in Washington, in 1953; in the Palace of the Legion of Honor in San Francisco, in 1956; and later at Yale, Notre Dame, and other universities.

The jury of the Biennale of Sao Paulo in Brazil awarded him in 1955, the international first prize for woodcuts, as well as the title "Best Woodcut Artist of the Exhibition." Steinhardt's talent had at last received international recognition.

Two years later an exhibition of his work took place at the Stedelijk Museum in Amsterdam, and he was invited to participate in the International Biennale in Tokyo. In 1958, several important exhibitions of Steinhardt's work took place in the Kunstmuseum in Düsseldorf, Germany; in Atlanta, Georgia; in Bogotá, Colombia; and in the Museum of Modern Art in Sao Paulo, Brazil. Steinhardt was also awarded a prize by the Arte Lithurgica at the Biennale in Venice, in 1958.

Three monographs have been published about Steinhardt: one by Dr. Hans Tietze in 1928; another, with a preface by Dr. F. Schiff, Director of the Museum of Modern Art in Haifa, by the Jerusalem Art Publishing Society; and a third, in 1959, by Dr. Leon Kolb of San Francisco, California, who also published a complete catalog of Steinhardt's woodcuts with an introduction and appreciation by this writer.

Although this is a book about Steinhardt's graphic art, a few words must be added about his paintings. From the Pathetic period up to today, he has never lost command of the palette and brush. We find in his paintings a tendency toward composition on a vast scale and a vivid and vigorous sense of color. They have an earthiness and elemental quality that are somewhat surprising when compared to his graphic work, most of which is permeated with fantasy and spirituality.

Steinhardt's capacity for empathy, his penetration into his theme, have always kept abreast of his technical ability. There is always a close and constant rapport in his woodcuts between theme and technique, and instead of the somewhat crude and coarse carving of his earlier years, which possessed a prototypal quality but lacked the subtlety that he achieved later, his method became delicate, more colorful, evincing respect for every detail in the wood, which in the brief instant it is attached to the sheet turns light into darkness and darkness into light. Steinhardt does not reproduce Nature; he lays bare its hidden soul, breathes into it, as it were, another soul that complements its own and explains its being, personally and universally.

There have been four distinct periods in the development of Steinhardt's graphic art—that of the Pathetiker, then the Lithuanian drawings, then the years of emotional realism born of his conflict with Palestinian life and landscape, later resolved in his growing affinity with the biblical present and past (though there are also in this period works reflecting the artist's storm-tossed fantasy, devoid of any contact with reality and even constituting a rejection of reality), and finally his surrealistic period, in which he produced imaginative landscapes and compositions, which, though unrelated to reality, nevertheless express more than is immediately apparent—far more than Steinhardt, in his earlier years, could express deeply and personally, but which, for those who can read the language he speaks, is abundantly clear. This final phase presents a mingling of strikingly figurative elements with deductive abstractionism, still related to a theme but at the same time increasingly outdistancing it, to achieve a drama that, though invisible, appears throughout his work.

To this period belong the woodcuts treating of biblical themes, not interpretatively now but suggestively, in which the artist hints at the dramatic encounter between man's spirituality and the tragedy of his environment.

Today, at seventy-six, Jakob Steinhardt is in the finest creative phase of his great talent. His latest works express a great calm, a rich experience of life. They have none of the harshness of the earlier ventures into the realm of the woodcut, though they have the same freshness. Despite his success—he is now represented in many important art collections in Europe and America—Steinhardt has remained a modest person, an artist faithful to his calling, carrying his mission to the world, preferring things spiritual to wordly pursuits. Endowed with a profound understanding of life, Jakob Steinhardt is an artist whose inspired work never ceases to exhort man to kindle that divine spark that dwells within him.

HAIM GAMZU

CATALOGUE

MONOTYPES

1. NUDE
   Chalk. 50 x 38.5 cm. 1907.
   Correction by Lovis Corinth on the right side.

2. NUDE, STUDY OF AN OLD MAN
   Chalk. 52 x 30 cm. 1907.

3. RECUMBENT NUDE
   Graphite. 20 x 28 cm.
   Paris, 1910.

4. STANDING NUDE
   Graphite. 32 x 20 cm.
   Paris, 1910.

5. THE LAST DAY
   Sketch for a painting.
   Ink and watercolor.
   20 x 18 cm. 1912.

6. THE FLOOD
   Sketch for a painting.
   Pencil, ink, and watercolor.
   32 x 42 cm. 1913.

7. SKETCH
   Design for a poster for the first exhibition of the "Pathetiker" in the Sturm Gallery in Berlin.
   Brush and ink. 44 x 31 cm. 1912.

8. LUDWIG MEIDNER
   Chalk. 27 x 20 cm. 1912.

9. PORTRAIT OF THE WRITER FUCHS
   Graphite. 22 x 17.5 cm. 1913.

10. IN THE BERLINER HOCH-BAHN
    Chalk and watercolor.
    55.5 x 45.5 cm. 1913.

11. HERMIT
    Pastel. 63 x 49 cm. 1912.

12. WINTER
    Charcoal, watercolor, and wash.
    20 x 15 cm. 1916,

13. LITTLE TOWN
    Chalk and wash. 20 x 15 cm. 1916.

14. OLD MEN IN VILLAGE STREET
    Chalk, heightened. 27 x 24.5 cm. 1920.

15. SMALL STREET
    Sketch for a woodcut.
    Charcoal, ink, and watercolor.
    36.5 x 26.5 cm. 1922

16. YONA'S CALLING
    Sketch for an illustration for the book Yona.
    Brown chalk. 27 x 24.5 cm. 1927.

17. YONA IN NINEVEH
    Sketch for an illustration for the book Yona.
    Brush and ink.
    24 x 18 cm. 1927.

18. SMALL-TOWN JEWS
    Charcoal. 24 x 34 cm. 1931.

19. GROUP OF BEGGARS
    Charcoal and watercolor. 19 x 26 cm. 1932.

20. JERUSALEM, SKETCH I
    Ink and wash. 24 x 26 cm. 1940.

21. JERUSALEM, SKETCH II
    Ink and wash. 15 x 23 cm. 1934.

22. EXCITED PEOPLE
    Charcoal and watercolor wash.
    27 x 22 cm. 1945.

23. GROTESQUE NO. 10
    Sketch for a woodcut.
    Ink and watercolor. 30 x 22 cm. 1952.

24. YONA SPIT OUT
    Sketch for a woodcut.
    Ink and watercolor. 26 x 38 cm. 1951.

25. BEGGAR'S VILLAGE
    Charcoal, ink, pastel, and watercolor.
    44.5 x 59 cm. 1957.

DRAWINGS

26. DRUNKEN MEN
33 x 24 cm. 1947.
27. GROTESQUE
24.5 x 30.5 cm. 1950.
28. GROTESQUE
Sketch for a woodcut.
19 x 29 cm. 1952.
29. STORM
Sketch for a woodcut.
32 x 41 cm. 1952.
30. RESTING BEDOUINS
Sketch for a woodcut.
42 x 49 cm. 1954.
31. SUNRISE
Sketch for a woodcut.
28.5 x 36 cm. 1954.

32. DEAD TREE
Sketch for a woodcut.
30 x 42 cm. 1956.
33. STORMY SEA
Sketch for a woodcut.
29 x 38 cm. 1952.
34. BEGGARS ON THE WALK
Sketch for a woodcut.
23.5 x 39 cm. 1957.
35. BIBLICAL SCENE
31 x 26.5 cm. 1959.
36. SAUL
39 x 28 cm. 1959.
37. NAOMI AND RUTH
40 x 30.5 cm. 1959.

LITHOGRAPHS AND ETCHINGS

38. HEAD
Lithograph. 11.2 x 5.5 cm. 1913.
39. ILLUSTRATION TO *MUSICAL TALES*
BY I. L. PERETZ
Published by Fritz Gurlitt Verlag, Berlin, 1920.
Lithograph. 22 x 16.5 cm. 1919.

40. PESTILENCE, AFTER AN OIL PAINTING
Lithograph. 18.8 x 25 cm. 1914.
41. HEAD OF AN OLD MAN
Verni mou. 15 x 19.5 cm. 1907.
42. VILLAGE
Verni mou. 15 x 19.5 cm. 1907.
43. HOUSE OF PRAYER
Drypoint. 17.5 x 12.5 cm. 1912.
44. ADORATION OF THE SHEPHERDS
Drypoint. 14 x 17.5 cm. 1912.

45. JEREMIAH
Drypoint and roulette. 12.5 x 11 cm. 1912.

46. CAIN
Drypoint and roulette. 11.7 x 14 cm. 1912.
47. HEAD OF A JEW
Published by Graphisches Kabinett, J. B. Neumann, Berlin, 1913.
Drypoint. 11.8 x 8.9 cm.
48. WINTER
Published by Graphisches Kabinett, J. B. Neumann, Berlin, 1913.
Drypoint. 11 x 14.3 cm.
49. HEAD WITH LANDSCAPE
Published by Graphisches Kabinett, J. B. Neumann, Berlin, 1913.
Drypoint, 8.5 x 8.5 cm.
50. POGROM
Published by Graphisches Kabinett, J. B. Neumann, Berlin, 1913.
Drypoint. 13 x 19 cm.
51. SMALL STREET IN Z.
Drypoint. 17.5 x 23.5 cm. 1918.
Published by Euphorion Verlag, Berlin, 1918.
52. WAR REMEMBRANCE
Drypoint. 22.2 x 18.2 cm. 1920.

53. CONVERSATION
Published by Euphorion Verlag, Berlin, 1921.
Drypoint. 16 x 11.5 cm. 1921.

54. FUNERAL
Published by Euphorion Verlag, Berlin, 1921.
Drypoint. 15 x 19.5 cm. 1921.

55. FAMILY
Drypoint. 18 x 13.7 cm. 1921.

WOODCUTS

56. ROCKY LANDSCAPE
14.1 x 14.5 cm. 1911.

57. LOVERS
9.3 x 12.5 cm. 1912.

58. LOVERS AND ROCKY LANDSCAPE
21.5 x 16 cm. 1912.

59. GIRL AND DEMON
23.5 x 17.5 cm. 1912.

60. THE MOURNER
18 x 16.5 cm. 1913.

61. JEREMIAH
17.3 x 13.6 cm. 1913.

62. CHRIST
Color woodcut. 16.2 x 12 cm. 1913.

63. HEAD
16.9 x 12.2 cm. 1913.

64. PAUL ZECH
21 x 14 cm. 1913.

65. HOMELESS
11.5 x 16.5 cm. 1918.

66. DEATH
27 x 24.5 cm. 1919.

67. WINTER
Published by Fritz Gurlitt Verlag, Berlin, 1921.
32 x 27.5 cm.

68. VILLAGE IN LITHUANIA
18.7 x 28 cm. 1919.

69. HAGGADAH ILLUSTRATION
Published by Ostertag Verlag, Berlin, 1920.
15.5 x 18 cm.

70. MORNING
14.8 x 18.8 cm. 1920.

71. FUNERAL
30.1 x 36 cm. 1922.

72. FAMILY OF DEMONS
23.5 x 28 cm. 1923.

73. DEMONS IN THE MOONLIGHT
30 x 34. 1923.

74. ILLUSTRATION FOR *JESUS SIRACH*
Published by Soncino Gesellschaft, Berlin, 1929.
15.5 x 12.5 cm.

75. ILLUSTRATION FOR *JESUS SIRACH*
Published by Soncino Gesellschaft, Berlin, 1929.
15.5 x 12.5 cm.

76. SELF PORTRAIT
40 x 30.5 cm. 1923.

77. GATHERING AROUND THE STOVE
40 x 50 cm. 1923.

78. SHABAT AFTERNOON
40 x 50 cm. 1923.

79. THE CALL
For the book *Yona*. 1923.
Published by the Jewish Publication Society, Philadelphia, 1951.
13.4 x 18.2 cm.

80. THE STORM
For the book *Yona*. 1923.
Published by the Jewish Publication Society, Philadelphia, 1951.
24 x 18 cm.

81. SOUNDING THE SHOFAR
Color. 27.5 x 17 cm. 1925.

82. IN THE SCHOOLHOUSE
Color. 53 x 43.2 cm. 1925.

83. ENTRANCE TO THE HOUSE

PLATES

1. NUDE

2. NUDE, STUDY OF AN OLD MAN

3. RECUMBENT NUDE

4. STANDING NUDE

5. THE LAST DAY

6. THE FLOOD

7. SKETCH

8. LUDWIG MEIDNER

9. PORTRAIT OF THE WRITER FUCHS

10. IN THE BERLINER HOCHBAHN

11. HERMIT

12. WINTER

13. LITTLE TOWN

14. OLD MEN IN VILLAGE STREET

15. SMALL STREET

16. YONA'S CALLING

17. YONA IN NINEVEH

18. SMALL TOWN JEWS

19. GROUP OF BEGGARS

20. JERUSALEM, SKETCH I

21. JERUSALEM, SKETCH II

1945

22. EXCITED PEOPLE

23. GROTESQUE NO. 10

24. YONA SPIT OUT

25. BEGGAR'S VILLAGE

26. DRUNKEN MEN

27. GROTESQUE

28. GROTESQUE

29. STORM

30. RESTING BEDOUINS

31. SUNRISE

32. DEAD TREE

33. STORMY SEA

34. BEGGARS ON THE WALK

35. BIBLICAL SCENE

36. SAUL

37. NAOMI AND RUTH

38. HEAD

39. ILLUSTRATION TO *MUSICAL TALES*

40. PESTILENCE, AFTER AN OIL PAINTING

41. HEAD OF AN OLD MAN

42. VILLAGE

43. HOUSE OF PRAYER

44. ADORATION OF THE SHEPHERDS

45. JEREMIAH

46. CAIN

47. HEAD OF A JEW

48. WINTER

49. HEAD WITH LANDSCAPE

50. POGROM

51. SMALL STREET IN Z.

52. WAR REMEMBRANCE

53. CONVERSATION

54. FUNERAL

12/30   Jakob Steinhardt 1921.

55. FAMILY

56. ROCKY LANDSCAPE

57. LOVERS

58. LOVERS AND ROCKY LANDSCAPE

59. GIRL AND DEMON

60. THE MOURNER

61. JEREMIAH

62. CHRIST

63. HEAD

64. PAUL ZECH

65. HOMELESS

66. DEATH

67. WINTER

68. VILLAGE IN LITHUANIA

69. HAGGADAH ILLUSTRATION

70. MORNING

71. FUNERAL

72. FAMILY OF DEMONS

73. DEMONS IN THE· MOONLIGHT

74. ILLUSTRATION FOR *JESUS SIRACH*

75. ILLUSTRATION FOR *JESUS SIRACH*

76. SELF PORTRAIT

77. GATHERING AROUND THE STOVE

78. SHABAT AFTERNOON

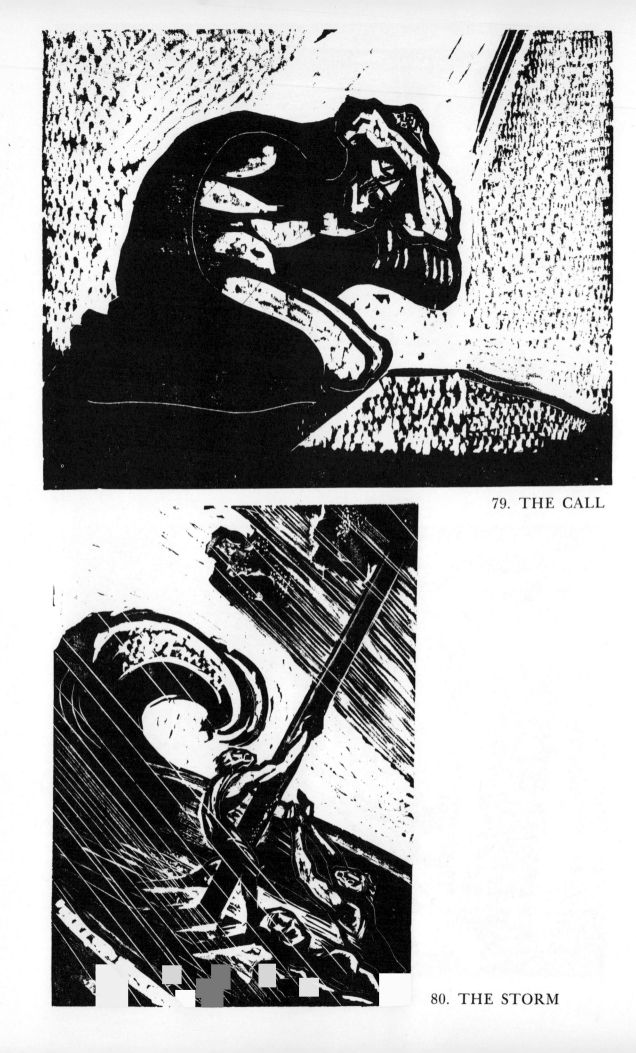

79. THE CALL

80. THE STORM

81. SOUNDING THE SHOFAR

82. IN THE SCHOOLHOUSE

83. ENTRANCE TO THE HOUSE OF PRAYER

84. ICE RING

85. BEGGARS IN THE STREET

86. OLD COUPLE AT THE WINDOW

87. MEA SHEARIM

88. STREET IN THE OLD PART OF JERUSALEM

89. ILLUSTRATION FOR
AGNON'S *THREE TALES*

90. ILLUSTRATION FOR
PATAI'S *KABALLA*

91. LANE WITH TREE

92. SIMCHAT TORAH

93. STREET IN OLD JERUSALEM

94. THE BLIND

95. SILENT STREET

96. OUTCRY

97. PROPHET WITH HEADCLOTH

98. YOUTH

99. DEAD ROOT

100. BLIND MAN

101. CAIN

102. THE EVIL

103. DREAM I

104. GROTESQUE NO. 9

105. GROTESQUE NO. 10

106. RESTING BEDOUINS

107. CREATION OF EVE

108. JERICHO

109. PRAYING BEDOUIN

110. THE PROPHET

111. CLIFFS AND BOATS

112. HOUSES BY THE SEA

113. RUINS IN MOONLIGHT

114. AQUEDUCT

115. VILLAGE IN GALILEE

116. VILLAGE WITH MINARET

117. JOB

118. OLD TREES

119. JEREMIAH

120. JUDEAN LANDSCAPE